East of York

Photographic Memories of Tang Hall, Heworth and Lawrence Street

First published 2006

ISBN-10 0-9552317-0-1
ISBN-13 978-0-9552317-0-4

Printed in Great Britain by
J.W.Bullivant & Son,
296 Bishopthorpe Road, York YO23 1LG

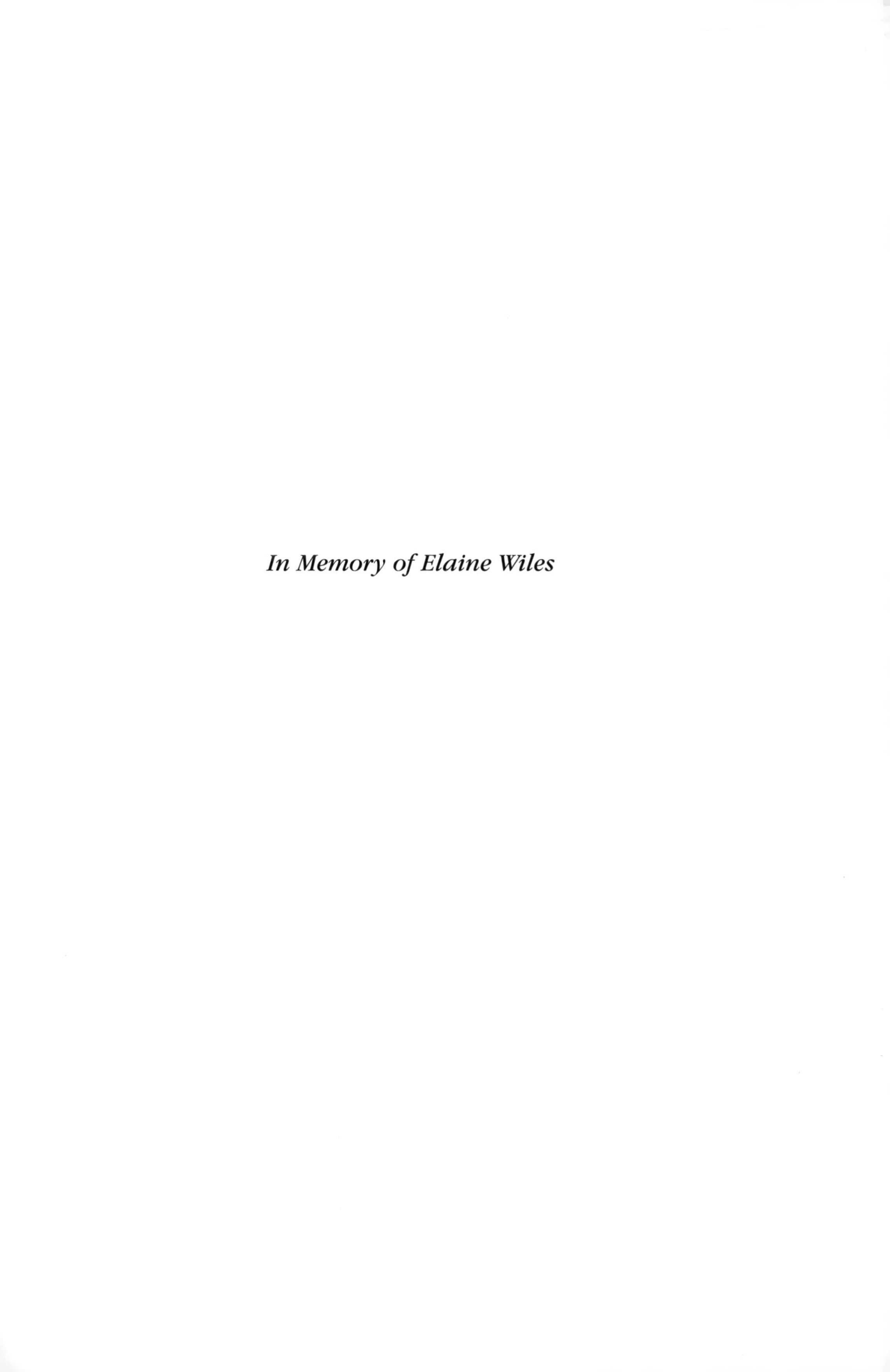

In Memory of Elaine Wiles

CONTENTS

ACKNOWLEDGEMENTS

We would like to thank all those who kindly lent us their photographs for this book. Thank you also to Neil Attisha of Grange Computers, Fossgate, Amanda Howard, J R Richards, Sue McCoey and her staff at Tang Hall Library and York Common Good Trust for all their help and support. Lastly, we are grateful to Local Heritage Initiative without whose support this book would not have been possible.

FOREWORD

It gives me great pleasure to introduce "East of York" by the Tang Hall Local History Group. The seeds of the book were sown in July 1999 when, as Local Studies Librarian for City of York Libraries, I was asked to set up local history groups in branch libraries across the city. From the first meeting at Tang Hall Library, it was clear that this was a group of individuals with a keen sense of identity and purpose. They were committed to recording and preserving the history of the area to the East of York. The group recognised that the richest material was held by the communities themselves and the main focus of their research was the photographs, memories and personal documents in their possession.

Their collection of material grew and in May 2000, the group was awarded a lottery grant to set up a Community Multi-Media Archive which would electronically store the photographs and documents they had obtained. This was put in Tang Hall Library so that it could be accessible to everyone and prompted further donations of records. Now with another lottery award, this archive is being made available in print.

The area to the East of York has not been the subject of any previous publication. Yet it is a microcosm of the suburban development that has taken place throughout York. Lawrence Street is an example of early development which occurred outside the city walls, along the main access roads leading into the centre. The proliferation of terraces spreading out from these main routes, is seen along Lawrence Street and Hull Road, while the establishment of housing estates, from the 1920s and 30s onwards, on previous country house lands and green fields, is also in evidence throughout the area. The foundation of the Tang Hall estate by the city council, initially to rehouse those living in poor conditions within the city walls, epitomises the drift of the population from the centre to the outskirts.

The photographs presented here, many of which are previously unpublished bring these facts to life. The majority have been found in family albums and present history through the eyes of the people who lived there. Because of this, it is a genuine local history, generated by the communities themselves. The book is a testament to the hard work and enthusiasm of the Tang Hall Local History Group. Hopefully it will inspire others to investigate their own local history and further increase our knowledge of the growth of York.

Amanda Howard

A Synopsis of
A HISTORY OF TANG HALL & ST. AELRED'S PARISH.
Written by Father Armand Carré , March 12th 1982

The name 'Tang Hall' may seem Chinese but in fact it's English.

The name derives either from the French word 'Étang' meaning a lake, or a pond, or more probably from the word 'Tongs', a fork made by the joining of the two becks which run through the area and into the River Foss along Foss Islands Road.

In the Middle Ages the area between Walmgate Bar and Layerthorpe was artificially flooded and stocked with fish to form the King's Pool. To the east of this artificial lake was the swampland called 'The Tang'. Nowadays it is difficult to imagine the area called Tang Hall to be a large swampy field stretching from Heslington to Heworth. It had only three houses situated along Tang Hall Lane, a Wind-Mill and a farm-house that is now a Post Office.

The northern beck flows through the eastern end of Stockton Lane and Appletree Village; the southern beck runs through Stamford Bridge, Murton and Osbaldwick Village. Their united waters wound their way through the 'Old Tip', now 'St Nicholas Fields', of bushes and rubbish before emptying itself into the River Foss. The land where the two becks join, was overlooked by the Manor, the Starkey family home, called 'Tang Hall': the Hall by the Pond, or the Hall at the Tongs. This Manor House was demolished in 1978.

The many floods in the area have demonstrated perfectly well what the Tang Hall area would have looked like at the turn of the 20th century.

After the First World War York City was becoming overcrowded and the York City Council purchased land from the Church Commissioners to build a new estate to the East of York. The Building of Tang Hall started in 1920 with part of Fifth Avenue and Carter Avenue. The sale of the Starkey's estate allowed the York City Council to buy the land and build between Tang Hall Lane and Melrosegate. A new world was opening up. People rushed to rent the new houses being provided by the Council. It was rewarding at last to be able to leave the slums of Walmgate and enjoy the new dwellings in the countryside, Tang Hall, a land of freedom between the becks.

By 1926 the slums of Walmgate were in the process of being demolished and nearly 1,000 new houses had been built in Tang Hall. The people longed for a community centre, a nucleus of social activities, a focal point to welcome everybody. That is why in Tang Hall something had to be done. Land was found in Flaxman Avenue. A community hut was proposed and a six-penny subscription per week was ordered; volunteers eagerly subscribed thus making the dream come true as quickly as possible. On 19th February 1927 Arnold Rowntree, the Lord Mayor of York, officially opened the Flaxman Club. The local Gazette emphasised the state of idealism and fraternity in Tang Hall.

THE BUILDING OF THE TANG HALL ESTATE.

At the end of the First World War (1918), the Ministry of Health issued a statement saying that due to overcrowding and unhealthy conditions, which were the main causes for the increase in the number of cases of Tuberculosis, in the majority of cities in England, cities like York should have a campaign to build new houses to alleviate the problems.

Thus it was decided at the beginning of 1919 to build a large estate of modern houses to the East of York on a large area of land unsuitable for agricultural use. The houses would be built to the classes A2,A3 & A4 standards set by the Ministry of Health. These included two and three bedroom semi-detached houses, three and four bedroom house in blocks of four.

York City council purchased 57 Acres of land North of the railway line in February 1919, and another 116 acres South of the railway line during 1920 and smaller plots of land in Glen (7 acres) and Heworth (83 acres) as the demand required.

Work started on the roads and drainage on the 28 July 1919.

The first phase of house building (185 houses) was split between two York companies, William Birch and F Shepherd.

The weekly rents were set at ten shillings, eleven shillings and six pence and thirteen shillings, dependant on the type and size of house (These rents were reduced by one shilling per week due to the large amount of unemployment in the City of York during 1922/4) A further four pence per week would be charged for a brick built tool shed. The rateable value (for the charging of electricity and gas) was set at seven pence and nine pence.

The first house (number 1) in Carter avenue was handed over, by the builders, to the Housing Authority on the 28 February 1921.

From the York City electoral register :-

1 to 32 Carter Avenue were fully occupied by the Autumn of 1921.

Followed by :-

Numbers 129 to 168 Fifth Avenue and Numbers 37 to 55 Fourth Avenue and most of Seventh Avenue in Spring 1922, Eighth avenue and part of Melrosegate in 1923, and Ninth and Sixth in 1924. The majority of this part of the estate was completed during 1925. Etty, Flaxman and Alcuin were completed in early 1926, Burlington, Constantine and Hewley in late 1926, Rockingham and Sterne in 1927. Asquith, Plumer, Tang Hall Lane and Wolfe in 1928-1930, Starkey & Cosmo in 1930. Hadrian and Woolnough were completed in 1929/30.

In all 22 contracts were issued to 12 different builders. A number of plots were sold to private house builders in the Tang Hall Lane and Burnholme areas.

In total 2214 (1780 by the Council & 434 by private builders) houses were completed between 1922 and 1936.

EARLY DAYS OF THE TANG HALL ESTATE

A view of the Heworth end of Fifth Avenue, taken from where Glen Garage is now.

LETTING OF HOUSES ON THE NEW TANG HALL ESTATE

(Yorkshire Gazette 10 July 1920)

The York Housing Sub-Committee have approved the following list of classes to have priority in the letting of houses on the Tang Hall Estate – when erected.

1. Men who have served in the forces during the war who are living in overcrowded conditions. Preference being given to those who are suffering a physical disability.
2. Widows, Mothers and Children of men who are serving or who have served during the war who are living in overcrowded conditions.
3. Persons with families living in apartments or in overcrowded houses.
4. Men in class 1 who have no homes of their own or are living in apartments. Preference being given to those who are suffering a physical disability.
5. Persons in class 2 who have no homes of their own or are living in apartments.
6. Persons recommended by the Tuberculosis Officer on grounds of urgent need owing to Tuberculosis in the family.
7. Persons under notice to quit, whose homes are urgently needed by the owners especially so recommended by a magistrate or a County Court Judge.
8. Persons in houses which will form suitable accommodation for those now living under insanitary conditions.
9. Young married couples not now occupying houses, or couples desiring to marry.
10. Former York residents who have had to give up houses during the war (other than service or ex-service men)
11. Persons(with families) living outside York but employed in York.
12. Other persons.

Class 1&2 refer to York residents or former York residents who have had to give up houses during the war.

The scheme is subject to the applicant being able to pay such rent as may be fixed by the City Council and is intended only as a guide to the Committee who reserve the right to decide in special cases.

Carter Avenue. The first Avenue to be occupied on the Tang Hall Estate in Autumn 1921.

Numbers 35 to 39 Seventh Avenue taken about 1925.

Horses at work on the Tang Hall Estate in 1929.

Houses while you wait on the Tang Hall Estate in 1927.

Fourth Avenue c.1930 looking towards Fifth Avenue.

Len & Harry Cole outside number 35 Fourth Avenue c.1930.

These horse drawn carts laden with hay pass the shops as they descend the railway bridge in Tang Hall Lane during the 1930s. This was a common sight during the summer when grass was cut in the meadows in the area now occupied by Penyghent and Whernside Avenues and the extreme end of Fifth Avenue including the site of Tang Hall Library and Clinic. Constantine Avenue on the left roughly follows the line of Green Lane which had existed from medieval times.

An early aerial view of the Tang Hall Estate showing the uncompleted Alcuin Avenue area.

A Modern aerial view of the Alcuin Avenue area of the Tang Hall estate.

A 1961 aerial photograph of the Tang Hall Estate with Burnholme school in the foreground.

Workmen pose for a photograph during the building of the Tang Hall Estate in 1929.

Heworth Church spire can be seen in the distant background of this photo taken in Melrosegate during the floods of 1933. The playing fields are on the immediate left and the rear of Cosmo Avenue on the right. Flooding occurred here regularly until Tang Hall beck was culverted and the Foss Barrier was installed. The submerged van in the foreground belonged to Arthur Lund Ltd, grocers of Monk Bar. The van in the background, which can be seen in the next photo, belonged to G E Barton.

This van can be seen in the previous photo and belonged to G E Barton, a very well known York firm of bakers with several branches throughout the city.

BUILDINGS

Tang Hall. This house, once the home of Captain and Mrs Starkey, became the Tang Hall Hotel. The building was demolished and the present Tang Hall pub and several houses were built on the site.

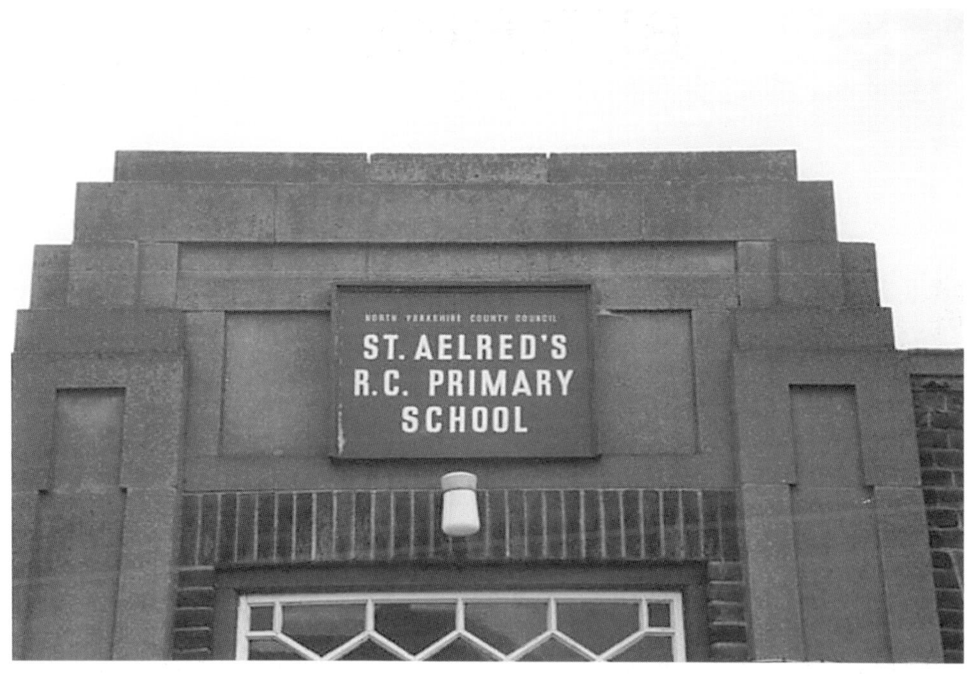

The Art Deco style stone portico of St Aelred's School, Fifth Avenue, before its demolition in 1987.

The entrance to St Aelred's primary school prior to its demolition.

The building being demolished was at one time a school run by the Society of Friends. One of its pupils was John Bright who later became a distinguished politician. One of John Bright's friends at the school was Samuel Tuke of the well known York family. The Tukes lived further along Lawrence Street in what is presently the St. Lawrence Working Men's Club. The school was established in 1823 and continued there until 1845 when it moved to its present address in Bootham.

Top of Melrosegate, seen from Green Dykes Lane, showing the Co-operative building.

Heworth Hall was a large family residence with upwards of fourteen acres of land with a dwelling house attached. When it was put up for auction in 1875 it was described in the Yorkshire Gazette as being an 'elegant mansion' belonging to Alderman Hargrove.

This house at 127 Lawrence Street, was St Lawrence's church vicarage.

Tang Hall Bridge, c.1900.

Tang Hall Bridge looking towards Heworth.

St Aelred's Church celebrated its 50th Anniversary in March 2006.

Tang Hall Library was designed to be one of a group of buildings intended to form a neighbourhood centre along with the Clinic. The cost of the building was £12,900. The library opened with about 7,000 books for adults; these included around 4,500 fiction specially selected to include the best reading to suit all tastes.

PEOPLE

Lawrence Street towards the end of the 19th century.
The young girl on the left is Sarah Wright (later Porter)
who was born in 1884 and lived to be a 100 years old.
Note the water pump and trough used by the animals
coming into the cattle market in Fawcett Street.

Sarah Porter celebrating her 100th birthday at the Bungalow hospital, Huntington in 1984.

These two young boys are Alfred Wright and his younger brother Frederick, born in 1894 and 1896. They were brought up in Lansdowne Terrace, Lawrence Street. Their sister (later Sarah Porter) is the girl pictured on Lawrence Street who lived to be 100 years old.

Len Baram as a small boy with his mother in a very rural Dales Lane, Heworth.

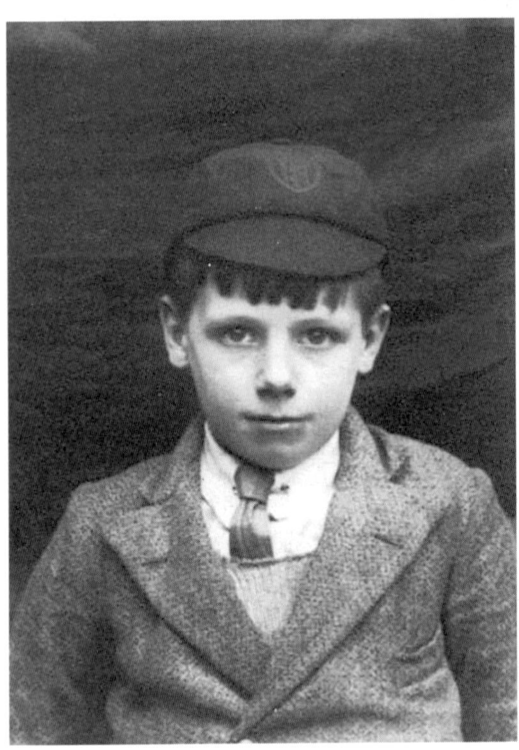

Len Baram, A young pupil of Tang Hall School wearing his school cap, 1930.

Reo and Maude Ankers at the gate of 31 Heworth Hall Drive. The house was named 'Gardena' as it had been built on the site of the kitchen garden belonging to Heworth Hall.

The Ankers family moved in to the newly built 31 Heworth Hall Drive in the early 1930's. They seem to have been a family who enjoyed entertaining and family gatherings.

This photograph shows Tom Caffrey and his two sons, Ken and James. They built many of the houses in Walney Road and Heworth Hall Drive. Walney Road was so named because Tom's wife hailed from Walney Island in Cumbria. The three also built the church hall on Melrosegate.

T. & M. CAFFREY

35 HEWORTH DRIVE

YORK

Houses for Sale from £495

BUILDERS

GENERAL REPAIRS TO PROPERTY

ESTIMATES FREE

TELEPHONE: HOUSE—2733 : OFFICE—2574

Caffrey's advertisement in the booklet announcing the opening of the Heworth Church Hall in October 1935.

Reverend Egbert Hudson stands in the centre of this photo in the doorway of St Lawrence Church with his two curates. Reverend Hudson's son Edmund became vicar of St Hilda's in 1956.

Canon McAniff, Parish Priest of St. Aelred's church with some young helpers after he had opened a fete, in 1969, at St. Hilda's church. On the right of the picture is Reverend Hudson, vicar of St. Hilda's.

Father T A Nolan, 1928. He was one of the first Curates to serve mass at the new St. Aelred's Church, Fifth Avenue, in the early 1930s.

P.C John Rowntree, pictured here with Miss World, was a familiar face on the streets of this area during the 1960s and 70s. Many will remember him on the school crossing patrol at the junction of Fourth Avenue and Melrosegate.
P.C Rowntree enjoyed being the village 'bobby' and the feeling of belonging. He retired in 1974.

PC Rowntree on his bicycle coming out of the Friargate entrance of the Police HQ.

Reo Ankers, a resident of Heworth Hall Drive poses with her bicycle . Note the criss-cross tape on the windows of the house in the background. This was to prevent them shattering in the event of a bomb blast during the Second World War. (1939-1945).

The Kelly family of Heworth pose for a photograph at the base of this old walnut tree in the late 1960s. This large tree once grew in the grounds of Heworth Hall. It still stands gracefully in the garden of a house in Heworth Hall Drive.

Fred and Alice Cole were the first tenants of 35 Fourth Avenue and lived there for many years bringing up a family of four boys. Fred was a keen gardener and Alice baked her own bread as did many women of her generation.

Early days in Hull Road Park – Joyce and Eileen Probert with their mother and Aunt Margaret. In March 1925 the parks committee agreed a scheme for creating Hull Road Park and its formal opening took place on Saturday May 2nd 1927 by the Lord Mayor, Oscar Rowntree.

Buying an ice cream from Ernie Questa's cart in Flaxman Avenue.

Leonard Lockwood with his Son David in the back garden of 191 Fifth Avenue in 1933.

In 1954 George and Olga Woodcock opened their shop in Fourth Avenue. Mr Woodcock had previously worked as a manager for the Co-operative Stores but had decided to branch out on his own. Mr and Mrs Woodcock lived above the shop and will be remembered by many for the personal service they provided.

Bryan Woodcock, a talented youngster of Seventh Avenue, was the son of George and Olga. Many people will remember him for his outstanding achievements in sport. He died tragically in 1953 whilst playing in a football match.

Bryan Woodcock
Born March 25th 1937

In Memoriam

I have been asked to say a few words as a tribute to Bryan Woodcock and I feel privileged to do so. I was his headmaster for nearly four years and I know his sterling character and was most happy to have his confidence and indeed his friendship.

His achievement in school was most outstanding. He was known to the outside world for his unusual success in games, athletics and boxing. His peak performance would seem to be his Yorkshire honours in boxing, rugby and football all in one year, possibly not equalled by any other boy in the country.

But we know more of him than even this and something that in my opinion was even greater.

Although he knew his ability he was never boastful. He was truly humble and played under another's captaincy.

In a final word, he was solid, friendly, most able and cheerful and he played the game of life, most nobly.

Signed
Herbert Wroe MA
Headmaster The Manor C of E Secondary Modern School, York
March 25th 1953

Tribute to Bryan Woodcock at his funeral service on the 25th of March 1953 by his headmaster, Herbert Wroe, MA.

George Ward was a cycle dealer and repairer who had his business at 65 Heworth Road. As well as selling and repairing bikes he supplied wireless accessories and charged accumulators. He is pictured here during the celebrations in Harrison Street for the Queen's Coronation in 1953.

Joan Freeman and Bernard Roberts marry at St Aelred's Church on the 8th of September 1954. This first church of St Aelred's eventually became the school hall when the present church was built in 1956.

This calendar was issued by the National Savings Committee and was painted by a Glen School pupil in 1944. The National Savings Committee was set up during the war to encourage people to save money. Certificates were issued in various denominations, many being redeemed at the end of the war.

Mr Edwin Bristow delivering milk in Lawrence Street.

Peter Bristow Memories

Moor Farm Dairy, c.1920

From small beginnings with a few cows which were kept and reared in fields off Bad Bargain Lane, a thriving dairy and milk business was established. The family then moved to Moor Farm, Murton and expanded the business. The area covered by the milk-round was Hull Road, Lawrence Street, Tang Hall and Heworth. The milk was originally delivered by cycle and horse with trap. Ellis Bristow (Snr), head of the family used the trap. After the death of Ellis following a fall from the trap in 1931, a milk van was used by his son Edwin Bristow and his older sister, Hilda. After the day's deliveries, canvassing for new customers took place around the new houses being built on the Tang Hall Estate. At the outbreak of war (in 1939), Edwin Bristow enlisted for military service and his deliveries were taken over by Frankie Bristow.

After the death in 1951 of Ruth Bristow who had run the dairy and farm following the death of her husband Ellis in 1931, the dairy moved to Heworth Road and the business was carried on by Hilda who was well known in the area. Hilda died in 1965 aged 68 years having worked up until her death.

CHURCHES AND CHOIRS

Interior of St Hilda's church before it was demolished.

An artists impression of the proposed original St. Hilda's church on Tang Hall lane. The church was never actually completed to this design.

This is a photograph of St Hilda's Church as it was actually built in the 1930s. It was demolished in 2000. The new church built on the same site is a dual purpose building used for services and community groups, Some of the original church land has been used for a new housing development.

The medieval church of St. Lawrence of which only the tower remains today. The rest of the building was demolished when the present church was built in 1883.

Inside the old St. Lawrence's church.

Interior of the present St. Lawrence's church.

Heworth church Choir.

Procession into St. Hilda's Church, c.1935.

Girl Guides line the route for Reverend Cosgrove and his wife on the occasion of St Hilda's Church Bazaar in 1935.

Presentation of a clock to Ron Heppell to commemorate 60 years as a chorister with the St. Lawrence's church choir.

St Lawrence's church choir pictured with the Archbishop of York, Cyril Forster Garbett.

Heworth church Choir.

Interior of the first St. Aelred's church which later became the school hall when the present church was built in 1956.

St Lawrence's church choir.

St Lawrence's male voice choir.

HEWORTH VOLUNTARY PRIMARY SCHOOL

HEWORTH CHURCH SCHOOL HEWORTH ROAD YORK

This school opened in 1873 in a building erected with the aid of a government gant. Boys, Girls and Infants were accommodated in 2 schoolrooms and a classroom. The fees were 2d and 3d for Boys, 2d., 3d., and 4d for Girls and 1d and 2d for infants. There were 2 mistresses. In 1877 the average attendance was 140. In 1897 when the first annual government grant was received the school had accommodation for 314 children and the average attendance was 183. In 1910 there were 2 departments, mixed and infants. After reorganization in 1932 there were Junior mixed and Infants departments in which the average attendance was 187 in 1938. The school continued as a voluntary aided Junior and Infant school after 1950. 90 children were enrolled after 1956.

This information is taken from 'A History of Yorkshire: City of York' Schools and Colleges.

Researched by ex pupil W. Maddison 1936 - 1942.

Heworth Voluntary Primary School

Heworth School pupils are photographed here in 1932. The detached house in the background was demolished and replaced by a more modern property. Heworth Methodist church spire can also be seen.

Heworth School re-enactment of a 19th century class room.

St. Aelred's Nursery 1967.

A music lesson at St. Aelred's school in 1969.

St. Aelred's Infants 1970.

St. Aelred's – The retirement of Miss Bankes, a well known and respected teacher.

St. Lawrence's standard 4 with Miss Porteous Headmistress of the girls' school far right.

St. Lawrence's girls reception class 1948/9. Their classroom in the old school can be seen in the background.

Tang Hall School in the 1960s.

Tang Hall Infant School Teaching staff - 1960s.

Tang Hall School top class 1953. With Mr Baxter Headteacher on the right.

Tang Hall School mid 1950s.

A class at Tang Hall School.

Burnholme School class 4a, one of the first classes to move from Tang Hall Senior School., c.1950.

A class of Derwent School in 1935.

Heworth School Choir

A class from the Avenue School in 1949 with their teacher Miss Shaw.

Flaxman Avenue Pavilion used as a school in 1933.

GROUPS

Mrs Hannah Maria Skelton with six of her children in the front garden of 99 Alcuin Avenue, probably in the late 1920s. She was the first tenant of the property, the family moving in during February 1926. This house along with the rest of the block of four was demolished to make way for the entrance to Welborn Close in the early 1970s.

Earliest known photograph of Heworth Scouts (1st Eagle Patrol), 1921.

Heworth Scout group and their leader Margaret Smith seem very solemn in this photograph of 1926.

Heworth Scouts pose for a photograph at the bungalow, Muncaster. 1934.

Heworth Scouts photographed in 1938.

The Deputy Chief Scout chats to Heworth Scouts.

Beryl Easton, Miriam Vevers and Marjorie Harrison were all members of St Hilda's Brownies and are photographed here with their pack in 1938.

Outside St. Hilda's church.

A band of helpers at St. Hilda's Bazaar in the mid 1930s, with Rev. Cosgrove.

Children dressed for a procession pose outside St Aelred's Church.

The cast of St Aelred's Pantomime Group pose for the camera in their second pantomime, Aladdin.

St. Lawrence School Girls Dept. dressed for a performance of 'A Midsummer Night's Dream'.

This photograph in the 1920s was taken in St Lawrence's Churchyard, and shows girls of St Lawrence School in costume for a production of 'A Midsummer Night's Dream'.

Tang Hall ARP wardens in Hull Road Park 1940.

A Christmas fair at St Lawrence's church hall in the 1950s.

Sir Len Hutton with members of Heworth Cricket Club in the Assembly Rooms.

Christmas Party in the Pavilion, Flaxman Avenue in the 1930s.

Residents of Milton Street pictured before setting off on an outing to Scarborough.

An unknown Sunday School party In November 1950. The party was given by Mr & Mrs Smith prior to leaving for Australia.

CELEBRATIONS

Betty and Jimmy Harlow as "King & Queen" at the
1953 Queen Elizabeth II Coronation party for people of Woolnough Avenue.

The residents of Heworth enjoy a party for the Coronation on the 6th of June 1953. The event was held in the grounds of Walnut Villa and the children were entertained with a Punch and Judy Show, sports and a fancy dress parade.

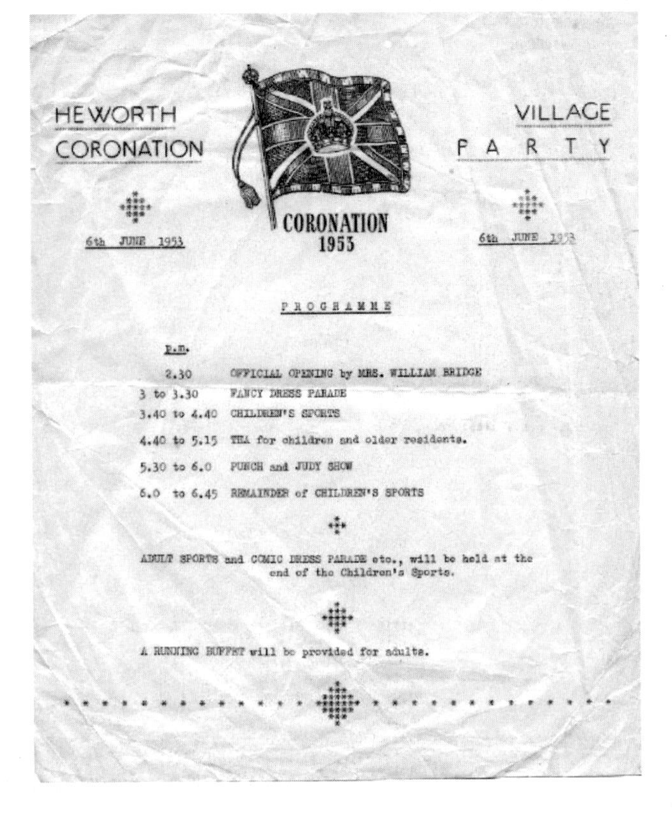

HEWORTH CORONATION VILLAGE PARTY

6th JUNE 1953

CORONATION 1953

6th JUNE 1953

PROGRAMME

P.M.

2.30	OFFICIAL OPENING by MRS. WILLIAM BRIDGE
3 to 3.30	FANCY DRESS PARADE
3.40 to 4.40	CHILDREN'S SPORTS
4.40 to 5.15	TEA for children and older residents.
5.30 to 6.0	PUNCH and JUDY SHOW
6.0 to 6.45	REMAINDER of CHILDREN'S SPORTS

ADULT SPORTS and COMIC DRESS PARADE etc., will be held at the end of the Children's Sports.

A RUNNING BUFFET will be provided for adults.

VE day party in Chaucer Street, 1945.

Queen Elizabeth II Coronation party in Chaucer Street, 1953. Pauline & Terry Stagnell in fancy dress.

Queen Elizabeth II Coronation party in Constantine Avenue, 1953.

Residents of Alcuin Avenue celebrate VE day in 1945.

George V1 Coronation party in Constantine Avenue.

Queen Elizabeth II Coronation party in Woolnough Avenue, 1953.

The younger children of Granville Terrace in fancy dress at their VE day party in 1945.

A group of older children dress up to celebrate VE day in Granville Terrace in 1945.

George V Jubilee Harrison Street party. Ladies competing in a race, 1935.

Herbert Street children in celebratory mood at their party for VE day, 1945.

Harington Avenue George V Silver Jubilee party in 1935.

Residents of Charlotte Street celebrate the Silver Jubilee of King George V, 1935.

Residents of Lansdowne Terrace celebrate V.E. Day, 1945. The building at the bottom of the street was the factory of Forster Coverdale the soft drinks manufacturers.

RECREATION AND LEISURE

A group of tennis players and friends relax in the garden of St Lawrence's vicarage, Lawrence Street, around 1930. The photograph shows Edmund Hudson (later to become vicar of St. Hilda's church) in the foreground.

Hull Road Park shortly after the opening in 1927.

An early photograph of a game of bowls in the Hull Road Park.

A 1950s view of Hull Road Park looking across the beck towards Millfield Avenue.

A view of Glen Gardens with Heworth church spire in the background.

1938 Tang Hall Junior School swimming class with Miss Rispin.

1947/8 The Avenue School football team - League A winners.

The Glen School Rugby team of 1946/47 celebrate after winning the Forster Todd Cup. Alexander William Forster Todd was well known in York rugby circles. He was chairman of York Rugby League as well as landlord of the London Hotel, Davygate. He was also Lord Mayor of York. The Glen School produced many good sportsmen and women.

Tang Hall School Athletics team with trophies.

1936/7 Derwent School football team.

1937 Derwent School football team photographed in Hull Road Park.

Heworth ARLFC are photographed in the grounds of the Tang Hall Hotel in 1952.

St Lawrence's church (married men's) football team.

St Lawrence's church (single men's) football team. These played a regular fixture against the married men.

1910 Heworth Cricket Club.

Opening of the Heworth Golf Club, Spring 1912.

1937/8 Inter-school sports at St Aelred's.

1974 1st Heworth Cedars (cub scouts) football team.

A FINAL STROLL DOWN MEMORY LANE

SEE THAT YOU GET

The BEST TABLE WATERS.

DRINK
FORSTER'S
DRINKS.

Sole District Agents for **VIMTO.**

Forster Coverdale & Co., Ltd.,

TELEPHONE 2282. **HULL ROAD, YORK.**

To Gardening Members

We carry a large stock of the following :-

POTS - all sizes

CANES - " "

LABELS - TWINE - RAFFIA, Etc.

LIME

MOST KINDS OF MANURES

Finest Scotch Seed Potatoes

Peas

Prize Winning Gladioli

AT KEEN PRICES

We sell to give you the benefit

ON SALE IN THE ALLOTMENT HUT ON SUNDAY MORNINGS and FRIDAY NIGHTS

Flaxman Pavilion advertisement for the Gardening Club.

“SOCIAL EVENINGS”

Before you buy that Bottle of Tonic See if we can chase your Blues away.

The finest way in which to Spend a Saturday Evening is to join the Merry Throng at the Pavilion.

Five Hours of Good Fun, in good Company.

For particulars, enquire of your Local Committee man.

WHIST DRIVES.

A Whist Drive is held in the Pavilion every Tuesday Evening.

Admission 9d.

SPLENDID PRIZES.

Remember a Whist Drive is a “Keep Fit Class” for the Brain.

A. HODGSON,

277 Melrosegate,

194 Tang Hall Lane, "Post Office,"

14 Lawrence Street,

NEWSAGENT, SWEETS, &c.

TOBACCONIST, Wholesale and Retail.

Place your Order with your Local Newsagent.

SUNDAY PAPERS DELIVERED.

PROMPT ATTENTION TO ALL ORDERS.

A Grand Selection of High-Class Sweets and Chocolates.

A wide selection of BIRTHDAY GREETING CARDS
and YORK VIEWS in stock.

GIVE US A TRIAL AND WE GIVE

SERVICE
CIVILITY and
SATISFACTION.

TRY OUR DELICIOUS ICES.

CITY OF YORK PUBLIC LIBRARIES

TANG HALL BRANCH LIBRARY

Fifth Avenue

will be open for the Registration of Readers on

MONDAY - TUESDAY - WEDNESDAY

26th, 27th and 28th NOVEMBER, 1962

from 9-30 a.m. to 12-30 p.m. & 2-0 p.m. to 5-30 p.m.

THE LIBRARY WILL BE OPEN FOR BORROWING BOOKS at 9-30 a.m. on

FRIDAY, 30th NOVEMBER, 1962

and thereafter at the following times

Monday & Thursday 9-30 a.m. - 12-30 p.m. 2 p.m. - 5-30 p.m.

Tuesday & Friday 9-30 a.m. - 12-30 p.m. 2 p.m. - 8 p.m.

Wednesday & Saturday 9-30 a.m. - 12-30 p.m.

Readers holding current York Library Tickets may use them at this branch

Printed in Little Stonegate, York, by Noel Richardson & Co. Ltd.

AT ALL TIMES BRING

YOUR REPAIRS TO

H. ATKINSON,

BOOT & SHOE REPAIRER

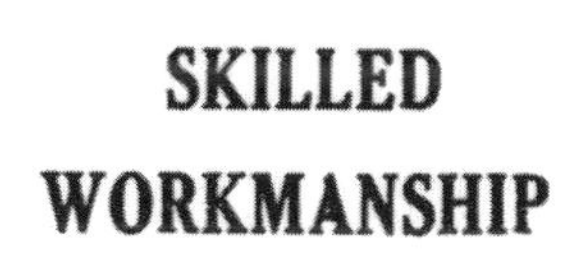

MODERN MACHINERY

277a, MELROSEGATE,

HULL ROAD, YORK.

Repairs neatly executed

Orders collected and delivered daily.

PRIVATE ADDRESS:

27, CARTER AVENUE,

HEWORTH, YORK.

Memories of Tang Hall

Bill Heppell

The houses on Tang Hall Lane from Osbaldwick Lane to Hull Road were very pleasantly situated; there were open fields at the back (until Hadrian Avenue and Woolnough Avenues were built) and open fields in front; we called the field opposite Goodrick's Orchard. Tang Hall Lane was a country road with old trees and only occasional street lighting. Millfield Lane was the same with only a few scattered houses and it was a long walk to Fishergate School until I was old enough - at about eight - to be allowed to cycle to school.
Thursdays and Mondays were hazardous, there were droves of cattle and sheep from the Corporation Farm at Osbaldwick to the Cattle Market on Fawcett Street and, of course there were the tram-lines from the Beeswing Hotel to Walmgate Bar.

Marjorie Todd (nee Hartas).

My parents moved into No. 5 Flaxman Avenue in 1926.
The estate was only just being built, there were no roads so our furniture had to be taken to Millfield Lane and carried across a field, over a plank across the Osbaldwick beck and up the fields at the other side That beck and the field nearer the houses later became part of the park.
I think our house must have been one of the first to be occupied as I can remember Alcuin, Etty, Constantine and Burlington Avenues being built.
There was no church for a long time although we did get a Parish Priest, Rev. Horrocks, who lived in Fifth Avenue. When enough money had been raised the first of the wooden buildings was built where the church was later erected and consecrated on the 22nd September 1934.

An unusual vehicle promoting the 'James' van, a cheap form of transport.

Milk deliveries in bygone days.

Extracts from the Glen School Magazine

GLEN GIRL - Audrey Larcum
I'm just a young girl from the Glen.
Trying to write with my pen.
A few lines that will rhyme
And all in good time
Might get my name in "The Glen".

THE LAST TOP CLASS IN GLEN SCHOOL - Delia Guild

Top class and Standard IV have moved over to the Tang Hall Senior wing, and they have moved to a lovely new school at Burnholme.

We have each got separate desks which we all like very much. There is a museum in our classroom where we have old Roman pottery etc. There is also an aquarium on our teacher's table and a cadis fly hatched the other day. Our classroom is always decorated nicely with flowers and plants which come in every day. When it is playtime we have the playground to ourselves, with plenty of room to play rounders. Most of us are leaving school this year which will be called Tang Hall Primary after the Summer holidays.

Good Luck -P Gibbs.

For twenty two years Glen School has been a happy family. From the opening of the school in 1928, when we occupied one of two wings of the unfinished building. Miss McIntosh and her staff set our aims high and ourselves along the busy tracks of worth-while ways.

Later, Mr Baxter carried on and developed the work so ably begun.

BOYS AND GIRLS, we could have had no finer Head. You, too, in your daily tasks must be fine and splendid. As our leavers build on the Glen tradition in their new schools, we who are left facing new outlooks must keep our wagons hitched to the stars, and our feet in splendid ways.

After the holidays our Infants and their Teachers are moving to another wing. It is with a feeling of great loss that we watch them go. But they are "just over the garden hedge" and we hope to see them often. Our best wishes for happy days go with them.

Good Luck. Glen, Old and New!